40 MORE DEVOTIONS
that work with youth

edited by Geraldine Anderson

JBCE

The Joint Board of Christian Education
Melbourne

Published by
THE JOINT BOARD OF CHRISTIAN EDUCATION
Second Floor, 10 Queen Street, Melbourne 3000, Australia

40 MORE DEVOTIONS that work with youth

National Library of Australia
Cataloguing-in-Publication entry.

40 More Devotions that work with youth.

ISBN 085819 811 8

1. Youth—Prayer-books and devotions. 2. Devotional exercises.
I. Anderson, Geraldine, 1961 -   . II. Joint Board of Christian Education.

242.683

First printed 1990

Cover design and photo by Kelvin Young
Design by Pat Baker
Typeset by JBCE on Ventura Publisher in Zapf Calligraphic
Printed by Victorian Printing Pty Ltd   JB90/1920

INTRODUCTION

'Hey I'm editing another devotions book, sort of a son/daughter of *40 Devotions that work with youth*. Will you contribute to it? After all you're a youth leader with lots of creative ideas and experience in doing devotions. You are also a youth leader who understands young people and will write something relevant for the 1990's. So what do you say?'

That's how it all began this time. After the success of *40 Devotions that work with youth*, it was decided to write another 40. Sounds simple enough, but it isn't really.

Many youth leaders believe devotions are the things you make up while there's a break in the program of a youth group activity, or while the young people are at supper. One criticism of *40 Devotions that work with youth* is that the print of the book is not large enough and it is difficult to read while driving to youth group!

Within this book you will not only find 40 self-contained devotions for use with young people, but you will also find some help in writing, preparing, doing your own devotions. Please spend some time going through the training chapters. The devotions you write will be more significant and relevant to the young people you work with than any book's resource.

There are some devotions in this book which are more suited to 12-14/15 year olds. I have marked them with an * in the table of contents.

Good luck.

Geraldine Anderson

CONTENTS

*Devotions marked * are especially suitable for 12-14/15 year olds.*

PLANNING YOUR OWN DEVOTIONS

The important thing to remember about a devotion is that it is not something you tack onto a youth group program.

It should be a natural part of any youth ministry in the church and as an act of worship should be well planned.

Below are two models of how to plan a devotion

Starting with the Bible

Check the Lectionary. The Lectionary is the calendar which has Bible readings attached to each Sunday of the year and some other special days of the year. It is a resource used in most churches in Australia and around the world. Your minister is sure to have a copy, or you can buy one yourself (they sell for under $1.00).

The Lectionary is a great resource for finding Bible readings. The Lectionary will give you an Old Testament reading, a Psalm, a New Testament reading and a Gospel reading for each Sunday in the year, and each reading relates in some way to the others.

So if your youth group is meeting on Friday July 6, the next Sunday's readings might help you.

The Bible is the best place to start when writing your own devotions. That way you won't fall into the trap that many youth leaders are accused of: finding something you want to say and searching through the Bible to find something that will fit your message.

You will remain faithful to God's message if you use the Bible as a basis.

Therefore, say you choose Luke 10: 25-37 (The Good Samaritan). You will begin with a story Jesus told and your message will spring from that.

So your planning sheet may look like this:

1. Bible reading—Luke 10: 25-37
2. Present the reading in a dramatic form
3. Prayer about confessing the world's and our own inadequacies
4. Message about caring for all people no matter who they are
5. Small group work talking about:
   a) a time you were helped by someone
   b) how that felt
   c) times when you have helped others
6. Prayer for others
7. Song
8. Benediction

Using a theme

There are good reasons for using a theme and developing a devotion along those lines. For example, times of the year such as Christmas and Easter will have their own special significance. Added to that there are things that happen in young people's lives which are important to acknowledge:

- school holidays,
- movement from one year level to the next,
- exams,
- family celebrations,
- birthdays,
- death,
- parents,
- relationships.

If you can keep in mind these and other significant things when planning your devotions you will remain relevant. For example, when one of the young people in our group died in a road accident it was important to centre our material on what death is, how it makes us feel, what is the good news that the gospel brings and where is God in all of this. A hard topic but well worth the work.

Many youth leaders have also used the night's activity as a theme for their devotion. For example, they have run a fun night on spies and espionage and the devotion was about God knowing everything about us, using Psalm 139.

The ultimate in 'bad taste'

The ultimate in bad taste is when a youth leader thinks at the last minute about what he/she wants to say, and goes skimming through the Bible looking for a passage which might back up their point. Yours and the Bible's message will be weakened if you plan this way.

Songs in devotions are important. Within this book I have not suggested any specific songs as everyone has access to different kinds of music.

There are many good songs written by Australians and others, it may be worth your while to seek out new song books occasionally. Using the same old songs or only using choruses will limit the potential of your devotion. Don't disregard hymn books as a source of music. In the hands of some people, hymns can come alive.

PRESENTING A DEVOTION

Time and again it has been proved that a time of devotion within youth groups is essential. A devotion may be the only Christian message some young people hear, so it is important it is done well.

Below are some handy hints to remember when presenting a devotion.

Climate setting

- Set a climate that will enhance what you are doing;
- If you want to be meditative, turn down/off some lights;
- Clean up the area you will be using, clearing it of play equipment, rubbish etc.;
- Give time for people to settle down;
- Give time for people to transfer from one activity to another (e.g., supper to devotions);

- Arrange the area beforehand so that people will sit where you designate.

Upfront work

If you are doing a devotion, you will need to be at least competent in front of the group. Some handy hints for upfront work:

- Speak clearly and slowly;
- Don't fidget;
- Be in a position where you can see every member of the group and vice-versa;
- Resist yelling to gain attention;
- Have clear, concise notes;
- If using other people have an order of devotion so it flows smoothly;
- Be sincere;
- Share the upfront work around, amongst other leaders and group members.

IMAGES OF GOD

You will need:

☐ Examples of art work depicting God

☐ A large piece of paper for each person

☐ Felt pens, crayons, coloured pencils (whatever you have)

☐ Magazines, scissors, glue

PREPARATION

Gather together some pictures, slides or paintings that depict the way people see God. There are many art forms, painting, sculpture etc. which have been created over the years where people have depicted their image of God.

You will find pictures of a person with a halo, an image of an old man in the sky with a big white beard. Think too, about what your image of God is.

THE DEVOTION

Begin by singing some songs acknowledging God's presence.

Ask the group to talk with two or three other people about what they thought God looked like when they were children.

After a few minutes ask some people to report back what they had shared in the group.

Show the group the images of God you have collected, explaining that there are several interpretations about what and who God is. There are no right or wrong answers.

Read John 14: 6-11.

Then hand out the pieces of newsprint and explain to the group that you will give them 15 minutes to draw/create their own image of God. They are not to talk to anybody about it as it is to be their own image, but they can use any of the materials available.

After 15 minutes ask the members to find one other person and have them explain to that person what their image is.

Place the images all around the walls, then commend them to God in prayer. (If possible leave them there for a few weeks at least.)

Creator God,
We cannot see you, and sometimes some of us are not sure you are actually there. We seek you, please be real to us and accept these images, our thoughts of you. Amen.

You might like to finish with some lively songs.

Geraldine Anderson

EVERY NOW AND THEN I THINK ABOUT MY DEATH...

You will need:

☐ Pens/pencils and paper for everyone

NOTE

Be prepared to explain who Martin Luther King Jr was, and a little about his life. (Some may not know of him.)

THE DEVOTION

Explain that the devotion will focus on what is important to each of us as individuals.

Read the speech in the box below by Martin Luther King. The speech is from the book *King* by William Johnston © 1978, Star books, W.H. Allen & Co. Ltd. pp 241-242.

'Every now and then', he told the congregation, 'I think about my death'. His words brought a low murmur of surprise from the parishioners.
'I don't think of it in a morbid sense,' he qualified, smiling faintly. 'I ask myself what I would want said. If any of you are around when I have to meet my day ... I don't want a long funeral. And tell them not to mention that I have a Nobel Peace Prize. Tell them not to mention where I went to school. None of that is important. I'd like somebody to mention that day that ... Martin Luther King, Jr., tried to give his life to serving others...
I'd like for somebody to mention that day that ... Martin Luther King, Jr., tried to love somebody ...
I want you to say that day that ... I tried to be right on the war question...
I want you to be able to say that day that ... I did try to feed the hungry ...
I want you to be able to say that day that ... I did try in my life to clothe those who were naked ...
I want you to say on that day that ... I did try in my life to visit those who were in prison ...
Yes, if you want to say that I was a drum major, say that I was a drum major for justice! Say that I was a drum major for peace! And all of the other shallow things will not matter. I won't have any money to leave behind. I won't have the fine and luxurious things of life to leave behind. But I just want to leave a committed life behind.
That's all I want to say. If I can help somebody as I pass along ... if I can cheer somebody with a word or song ... if I can show somebody that he's travelling wrong ... then my living will not be in vain.

If I can do my duty as a Christian ought ... if I can spread the message as the Master taught ... then my living will not be in vain.'

Ask people to gather in small groups of three or four. Ask the following questions:

- What emotions does this speech raise?
- Have you ever considered if you died, who would come to your funeral?
- At your funeral what would you want said?

On the paper provided, have each person write an obituary or a eulogy for themselves. (You may need a copy of an obituary, in case people don't know what it is).

Ask the people to discuss what they have written in the small groups and discuss 'What have you learnt about yourself and what is important to you?'

Call people back into the large group and conclude with someone reading Deuteronomy 30:19. During the reading, light a candle as a symbol of life.

Conclude in prayer for people as individuals, the paths we choose in life and who we are.

David Guthrey and Jeff Jackson

OUT OF THE DARKNESS

You will need:

☐ A candle for every person

THE DEVOTION

Have the group sit on the floor in a circle, each with a candle. Turn out the lights and begin.

Leader: There are many names for the darkness that surrounds us. Isolation, struggle, exams, school pressure, fighting, tension, lack of friends...
What are the points of darkness in your life? Think of them now and if you want to, mention them in the group. Don't worry if you do not feel like speaking in the group.

Leave some time for silence. Whether people have spoken aloud or not, pray the following prayer.

Creator God, there are times when we do not understand this life or this world and the dark spots that surround us. Help us as we experience pain and darkness. Be with us as we struggle on. Amen.

Leader: It is better to light a candle than to curse the darkness.

The leader then lights his/her candle and passes the flame around the circle until all candles are lit.

Have someone read John 1:1-5.

Leader: Just as the darkness has many names, so too does the light. It brings with it many images of hope and strength. What are the points of hope and strength in your life? Think of them now and if you want to, mention them in the group.

Leave some time for silence. Whether people have spoken or not, pray the following prayer.

Creator God, we give thanks for the points of hope and strength in our lives. We celebrate the times of joy and when things go right for us. Help us to remember you are celebrating with us in our times of strength and joy. Amen.

Have someone read Isaiah 9:2-3.

Leader: The light shines in the darkness and the darkness has not put it out.

Finish with a song of hope.

Libby Renton

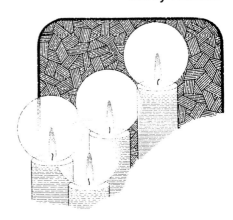

BURSTING RACISM

You will need:

☐ 1 black and 1 white balloon

☐ A pin board

☐ A pin

NOTE

This devotion is best done as a conclusion or introduction to a larger activity that is focusing on the issue of racism.

THE DEVOTION

Sing a few songs about servanthood, or being part of God's family.

Have a someone blow up both balloons and tie them in front of the group.

When the balloons are inflated divide into smaller groups of two or three. Ask the following questions:

- What is racism?
- What is discrimination?
- Are you racist?

If you have time you might like to ask groups to report back a few general answers to the questions.

Have the person who blew up the balloons now tie them together and pin them to the pin board. Ask people to focus on the balloons.

Leader: When we think about racism we need to remember that people of different races are still people. Look at the balloons. The same air is in them. They were joined together by the same person. The rubber, their skin, is made out of exactly the same materials. The only difference in these balloons is the colour of the pigment in their skins. The balloons are just like people. What is in one person is the same as in anyone else. All people have an equal capacity to feel sorrow, pain, joy and celebration.

Have two people alternately read the following readings:

>   Genesis 1: 26-28
>   Psalm 89: 8-14
>   Galatians 3: 26-29
>   Galatians 5: 16-17
>   Galatians 5: 22-25.

To conclude the devotion, burst the balloons as a symbol that one day racism will no longer exist.

Lead the group in prayer, remembering God's concern for all, particularly for the oppressed. Pray also that God will work through each of us as people of the Kingdom.

Mark Lawrence

JELLY BEANS

(suitable for 12-14/15 year olds)

You will need:

☐ One 250 gram packet of jelly beans for every eight people

NOTE:

The correct jelly bean flavours are:

Red—raspberry
Black—aniseed
Violet—blackcurrant
Pink—strawberry
Dark orange—orange
Yellow—apricot
Light orange—passionfruit
Green—lime
White—vanilla

THE DEVOTION

Place the jelly beans in a bowl and ask everyone to select one of each colour. If the group is small, go around the group and ask each person to identify what flavour each jelly bean is. If the group is large, break them up into smaller groups and get each group to report, after discussion, what flavour they think each jelly bean is.

The jelly beans are not to be eaten.

It is very unusual for anyone to get all the correct flavours. You might like to get them to write down their answers.

When they have shared their answers, tell them what the correct flavours are.

There are three obvious reasons why it is hard to guess the correct flavours of jelly beans:

1. We usually eat our jelly beans by the handful and can't possibly isolate individual flavours.

2. We are not used to thinking about what we do or eat.

3. We are not very observant.

Ask everyone to identify what category they fit into and tell the rest of the group.

(What you do now depends on where you want to take this devotion, two options have been provided for you)

Option 1

Leader: As with jelly beans, we often lump people together and fail to recognise individuality. As each jelly bean is different, so too is each person different. When we say things like:

all women are...
all Asians are...

we miss out on the richness and the variety that exists among God's people. We are lucky that God treats us as individuals and cares for each and every one of us.

Have someone read Matthew 10: 29-31.

Leader: As we are treated as valuable individuals, we have an obligation to treat others in the same way.

Pray for God's help in treating others as we ourselves would like to be treated and thank God for loving every one of us.

Option 2

Leader: We are constantly surrounded by the beauty of God's creation and yet pass it by each day, almost unaware of its existence, just as we eat jelly beans and don't know their flavour. Much attention and thought has gone into making jelly beans—what colours to use, what flavours to make—all this has been carefully considered. How much more complicated and beautiful our world is!

Have everyone go outside and find a flower or a leaf (or any natural thing), Ask them to study the object and then say something about it to the rest of the group.

Have someone read Psalm 8.

Close in prayer for the world.

Cliff Barclay

YUPPIES

You will need:

- [ ] The prepared tape (see below)
- [ ] Tape recorder
- [ ] Two people to read the 'Greed prayer'

PREPARATION

Find two or three people whom you perceive to have some wealth, and ask them the following questions, taping their comments.

1. If you were suddenly given $20,000 what would you do with it?

2. What is your idea of the perfect Sunday morning?

3. What are your favourite foods?

4. What do you do with your spare time?

THE DEVOTION

Play the tape you have prepared.

Ask the group some questions (either ask the questions in the whole group or break up into smaller groups for more participatory discussion):

- How many of you think the people on this tape are YUPPIES?
- What do you think about their answers to the questions?
- How would you answer these questions?

Have two members alternately read the following 'Greed prayer':

1. Dear God, It's good to know you're there when I need you. I need you tomorrow—desperately. I've been studying really hard and the big exam is really important. So please be there for me. It might mean the difference between credit and distinction, and boy would that open up some jobs for me.

2. Dear God, I really, really, really hope my football team wins tomorrow. They need all the help you can give. Give the coach the power to pull them up and trounce the other team. 'On ya God.

1. Dear God—my good mate! That little red sports car in the show-room is getting closer—it's begging me for a test drive! Please whisper a bit of generosity in my boss's ear next month when we're up for a salary review. I can't stand driving the old bomb I've got any longer—after all it's not safe.

2. God, please, please, please, let me win Tatts this week and I promise I'll put a third of the winnings in the offering plate next week—promise— Go on be a sport.

1. Dear God, help me to stop eating all that junk and lose some weight. I need your power, especially when we go out. I promise I'll never pig out on food again if you help me lose 2 kilos before I go to that party.

2. Dear God, get mum off my back please, she is such a pain. Thanks God, you're always there when I want you. Amen.

Read Matthew 6: 24-34.

Finish with the story in the box below.

Ask the following question of the group:

- Which do you believe in and serve, God or money?

Finish with a prayer or a song.

Elizabeth Grant

Which do we believe in and serve, God or money?

Some youth leaders from around the world were talking, sharing what they do in youth groups and what the church is like in their various countries. We heard from a youth leader from South America whose youth group activity was to encourage the young people to obtain their First Aid Certificates. Then when peaceful demonstrations in the streets were violently broken up by the army and the police, the youth group members would administer First Aid to the beaten and the tortured.

For those in countries like Australia, New Zealand and Britain, this type of youth group activity was very foreign.

But the South American youth leader had more surprises. To the Australian youth leaders he said 'I have much admiration for you Christians in this country. It would be very difficult to be a Christian here in Australia.'

'But we are not risking our lives as Christians like you are', was the reply. 'Surely it is more difficult to be a Christian in your country.'

'Oh no, not at all. Here in Australia you have many Gods. You have the God of materialism. You have housing, social security benefits for the unemployed, the sick. You have material possessions that keep people happy and amused. Your young people say that they do not need God here. They have all the money they need to sustain their lives.'

'That's true', replied the Australians.

'In my country if we do not believe that God is there, loving and caring for us, then we have nothing. We need God, and when we pray in the Lord's prayer, "Give us today our daily bread", that is exactly what we mean.'

MOVING ON

(suitable for 12-14/15 year olds

You will need:

☐ 3 clowns to act out the mime

☐ A bunch of flowers

THE CONCEPT

This devotion is appropriate when you have people leaving your group and going to an older group, or—with a little adaptation—leaving and going somewhere else. It is written to help the transition from one group to another.

PREPARATION

You will need to rehearse the mime so that the clowns know what to do.

THE DEVOTION

Have a stage or focus area that the clowns will use. Have those who are going to the older group sit on the edge of the stage or focus area. They do not know what will happen but are asked to participate when requested.

Read Matthew 28: 16-20.

THE MIME

The clowns enter and move about the stage on their own. They sit down and mime talking to themselves, being alone. Then they notice each other. With a little shyness at first, they interact with each other until they are laughing, playing and moving around together. They pick up flowers which are lying on the stage and give them to each other.

Clown 1 mimes being called away by a voice which the clown tries to ignore. Clown 1 continues playing. The voice becomes more insistent and the clown gets angry, then sad.

With sadness the other clowns in the group wish Clown 1 farewell and hand the clown all the flowers they have gathered. They wave to Clown 1 who departs to sit on the edge of the stage at the front. The other clowns take a while to readjust to losing their friend. They mime disappointment, sadness, bewilderment.

After a while they go into the rest of the group and invite some of them to join their group and soon they are playing again and gradually move to the back of the stage area.

Meanwhile Clown 1 has spent some time watching and feeling sad and left out. Clown 1 mimes feeling lonely and mimes giving the flowers away to nobody. Clown 1 notices the graduates sitting on their own at the side of the stage, at first the clown is too shy to approach them. The clown finally approaches the group and offers them flowers as a token of friendship. The graduates accept and soon Clown 1 and the graduates are laughing and playing together.

The other clowns and their group come to the front of the stage and offer a few members to Clown 1's group. All clowns then go into the audience and bring new members into their groups until everyone is on stage. All join hands in a circle.

Pray for those moving on:

Creator God, tonight we have to say goodbye to some friends who are going to another group. Thank you for all they have shared with us and watch over them as they move on. We pray that they will find again the friendship and fellowship that they have shared here with us. In Jesus' name. Amen.

Finish with a few songs.

Jennie Cooper

BELIEVE IT OR NOT

You will need:

☐ Enough blindfolds for one between two

THE DEVOTION

Put people into pairs and give them a blindfold. One person is to be blindfolded and the other is to take them on a walk around the area you are in. (Encourage people to go outside if they wish.)

Gather the group together and ask those who were blindfolded the following questions:

- What did it feel like being led around?

- Did you have faith in the person who was leading you?

Then ask of the whole group:

- What things do we do every day that require faith? (eg., drive a car)

Have someone read Hebrews 11:1-3.

Then ask the group:

- What does it mean to have faith in God without seeing God?
- Where can God lead us if we trust in God?

Have someone read Mark 11: 22-24 as a conclusion.

Michele Trebilcock

AROUND THE WORLD

You will need:

☐ A map of the world

☐ 1 large free standing candle and 6 smaller free standing candles

☐ Newspapers

PREPARATION

Before the devotion, break into six or more smaller groups. (One or two people in a group is fine).

Allocate each group a country of the world. They will be responsible for writing a prayer about that country.

Within their groups they are to think of that country and what issues it faces that may need prayer.

For young people who are unaware of the issues in the world, recent newspapers will help.

While the groups are working, arrange the room, placing the world map in the middle of a circle of chairs, the candle at the top.

Hand out a candle to each group.

THE DEVOTION

Begin by having people sit on the chairs in the circle. Don't make the circle too large: if there are not enough chairs, ask people to sit at the feet of those on chairs so that they are inside the circle.

Sing a few songs about the world, God and our responsibility in the world.

Read Matthew 5: 13-16.

Leader: What happens in the world is everyone's responsibility. If one part of the world is suffering, we have a responsibility to care and try to help. Lots of things that happen in the world are often the fault of the rest of the world. Some parts of the world starve because other parts of the world take too much food for themselves.

Jesus Christ taught that we are responsible for our brothers and sisters everywhere. That also means those thousands of miles away.

Let us pray for the world.

Read John 8:12. While this is being read, light the large candle at the head of the map of the world.

Then invite group 1 to come out, light their candle and read the prayer the group has written. When they have finished, they place their candle on the relevant country they are praying for.

The leader then reads the following reflection:

Dear God,
What are you doing with this world that you made
Where people are meant to be free?
As I asked him the questions and searched for his answers
He asked the same questions of me.[1]

Group 2 is invited to come forward and do the same as the first group. When they have finished, the leader again reads the above reflection.

The other groups come out in turn and read their prayer. After the final group (group 6) has placed their candle on the map the leader reads the following:

Dear God,
What are you doing with this world that you made
Where people are meant to be free?
As we ask him the questions and search for his answers
He asks the same things of you and me.[2]

A song may be sung here about the way God loves the world.

As a benediction read Matthew 28: 16-20.

Geraldine Anderson

---

1   From the song 'What are you doing?' by Tim Beale. Used by permission.

2   From the song 'What are you doing?' by Tim Beale. Used by permission.

RIGHT HERE WAITING

You will need:

☐ A copy of Richard Marx's song 'Right here waiting' (single EMI US 2266 or from the Album *Repeat Offender* EMI USA 790)

☐ A sheet of poster paper for each person

☐ Felt pens

☐ Four people to be involved in a sculpture which will 'sculpt' the Bible reading

PREPARATION

The people involved in the sculpture will need rehearsing and the process explained to the group before the devotion.

THE DEVOTION

Ask the group to sit in one big circle, putting the sculpture people in the middle.

Begin with a few songs.

Hand out paper and felt pens to everyone.

Read Luke 15: 1-32.

As you read Luke 15: 1-32, the four people sculpt the picture. The beginning of the reading has three people grouped together. A father-figure is on a chair holding hands with the two sons, who are linked as well.

As the reading progresses the sculpture changes, or is changed by someone else. Those in the sculpture become the parts of the story, e.g., pigs, farmers, city people and so on.

At the point where the younger son separates and leaves, pause in the reading and have the group write on their posters one or two things that could/does draw them away from God, from their family. (For example, popularity with friends, desire, money).

Have the group yell to the younger son to attract him to their placard.

As the son is experiencing rejection in the reading, the group turns their back on him.

The son walks over to the pig farmer.

The father-figure should strain towards the son all this time, while still keeping in touch with the older son.

When the reading reaches the point of the older son's anger, have the group turn their paper over and write what feelings they think they would have if they were the older brother.

Continue the reading to the end of the passage.

Finish with the older brother breaking contact and the father straining after him.

Leader: God never gives up on us, and whatever we do (no matter how guilty or low we feel), God welcomes us and reaches out to us.

Ask people to close their eyes and imagine that God is singing to them, then play the song 'Right here waiting'. During the song people may respond by reaching out towards the middle of the circle.

Finish with some silence or a prayer.

David Guthrey

PSALM 23

You will need:

☐ Pencils and paper for everyone

☐ The 23rd Psalm written up on newsprint

PREPARATION

If you can find a recording of the 23rd Psalm, if would be appropriate to play at the beginning of the devotion to get people settled and their minds on the words.

THE DEVOTION

Read Psalm 23 through once.

Read it through again, stopping at each verse to add the following comments.

Verse 1: The Lord is my best friend, who never lets me down.
Verse 2: God takes the heat off when I get stirred up.
Verse 3: God makes me feel alive and keeps me on the right track.
Verse 4: Even though things around me get pretty scary, I'm not scared because God's hand is on my shoulder.
Verse 5: God has filled my life with so many amazing things, much more than I deserve.
Verse 6: I am told that God will always care about me and love me to death. I will always be living with God who is my best friend for life.

Put up the newsprint with the 23rd Psalm written on it so that the whole group can see it.

Hand out pencils and paper.

In as much time as you have, ask the group to write their own version of the Psalm. Don't hurry them. (If you have a large group, you will need to break into smaller groups and let them work together on the Psalm.)

After appropriate time, have the group sit in a circle. Re-read the Psalm from the Bible and move around the circle so that each person/group can read out their re-written verses. This should be done prayerfully.

Another option is to break up the Psalm and give every person one verse each.

Finish with a spoken or sung benediction

Jennie Cooper

HOT PIZZA

You will need:

- [ ] One large hot pizza
- [ ] A candle
- [ ] Salt and pepper
- [ ] A knife
- [ ] Six readers to read the following Bible readings:
  John 8:12
  Matthew 5: 14-16
  Matthew 5:13
  John 6: 47-51
  Galatians 5: 16-26
  Revelation 3: 14-16

PREPARATION

Give out the Bible readings to the people who are reading (you may need to provide Bibles).

THE DEVOTION

Gather the group in a circle, sitting on the floor, and place the hot pizza in the middle of the circle.

Leader: We're sitting around a pizza tonight because I want to explain that even in the ordinary things in life, God can be seen and we can understand more about God if we are prepared to look around us.

(Light the candle.)

Candles light a room, flame also provides heat. Through flame and heat, life can be given to other things. We need light, flame, heat and food to sustain us.

(Have readers read John 8:12 and Matthew 5:14-16, then place the salt and pepper by the pizza and candle.)

Leader: We are called by Jesus to be the salt of the earth and God has put us here to flavour all things. We are called to influence the flavour and taste of all that is around us.

(Have reader read Matthew 5:13, then get the knife and cut the pizza.)

Leader: Jesus is the bread of life, Jesus sustains us and gives us life. We should live off the bread that Jesus offers. As I cut this bread, remember that Jesus's body was cut and broken for us.

(Have reader read John 6: 47-51.)

Leader: The different toppings on the pizza are like the different gifts that God gives to people. Everyone has different things to offer. Some call them the fruits of the Spirit. Every person is as important as another person, each person is unique.

(Have reader read Galatians 5: 16-26.)

Leader: The important thing to remember is with God you're either in or you're out. With Christianity there is no place for people who are lukewarm. You're either 'hot' or you're 'cold'. God needs all of you, God likes it hot.

(Have reader read Revelation 3: 14-16.)

Leader: Next time you eat a pizza, remember that even in the ordinary, God can be found.

Give thanks to God for food to sustain us and then eat the pizza.

Wayne Smith

AIDS AND US

You will need:

- [ ] Large sheet of newsprint
- [ ] Large sheet of clear plastic
- [ ] Black felt pens
- [ ] Coloured felt pens
- [ ] Newspaper headlines about AIDS

PREPARATION

Put the newspaper headlines about AIDS up on the large sheet of newsprint on the wall.

THE DEVOTION

Explain that the devotion is centring around the issue of AIDS and what that means for all of us.

Invite people to use the black felt pens and write on the paper any other things that come to mind when they think about AIDS. The words could be things like fear, pity etc. There will be many responses; there are no right or wrong answers.

Then seat the group in a circle around the clear plastic. Ask four different people to read the following readings. While they are reading, write the Bible passages in different coloured pen on the sheet of clear plastic. (If you wish you can write the passages out in full, or just the reference—it is up to you).

Psalm 8: 3-4
Psalm 139: 13-15
Genesis 1:27
Genesis 1:31

Have the group sit and face the wall with the newsprint. Ask someone to read out the statements that were made about AIDS on the paper.

Pray the following prayer:

Dear God who created us and all that is around us, we thank you for all your gifts, and we praise your creation. Help us, God, to understand now that part of the world you have created has a disease that kills. We are sometimes afraid of AIDS and afraid of those who suffer from it. You must be hurting, God, to know that your creation and your children are suffering. Help us to under-stand and to support those who need us.

Invite people to write on the clear plastic words of hope.

Gather up the clear plastic and place it over the sheet of newsprint, explaining that we do this to symbolise that we live in God's world and we live in the hope that comes to us in our relationship with God. We are all part of God's creation, sick and healthy.

Finish with a song on creation.

Heather McMinn

MEDIA CARING

You will need:

☐ Four or five newspaper cuttings of violence and death scenes.

☐ Four or five people to read the headings and a part of the article.

THE DEVOTION

As each cutting is read, the leader reads the reflection.

Read cutting one.

Leader: Watching someone die must be the most traumatic and horrible experience a person can go through, but I've seen many films in which people are murdered. When I was little it used to frighten me, now I know it's only 'the movies' or only 'television'. Now I'm not sure which is fact and which is fiction. Now I am de-sensitised to the violence around me.

Read cutting two.

Leader: What is the value of the human life? The world will spend thousands of millions of dollars saving animals from extinction while children still starve. What is the value of human life?

Read cutting three.

Leader reads Mark 12: 28-31.

Read cutting four.

Leader reads Romans 13: 8-10.

Finish in prayer about being aware that we are de-sensitised to suffering and that we need to remember that God still cares about us and other people.

Wendy McKenzie

BE STILL

You will need:

- ☐ 3 readers
- ☐ Torches
- ☐ A copy of the *Good News Bible*

PREPARATION

Clear the room of equipment and chairs. Prepare the room so that it will be as dark as possible when you turn off the lights.

THE DEVOTION

Sing a few lively songs which celebrate the presence of God.

Ask people to isolate themselves in the room. They need to be by themselves without touching anyone else.

Turn off the lights.

Reader one: Why is it so hard to take time out? Time to be, rather than time to do. Time to think, time to spend alone, time to spend with God, and especially be silent.

Reader two: There is always so much to do, so much that needed to be done yesterday and is still waiting to be done. It is so hard to fit everything I need to do into my busy life. How can I have time to be still? How can I have time to listen?

Reader three: Slow me down, God. Teach me to appreciate stillness. Continually remind me that there is more to life than rushing around filling up each minute with something to do.

Reader one: Help me to take time out.

Reader two: Help me to be still and know that you are there.

Reader three: Help me feel your peace in this busy world.

Leave some time for silence.

Reader one: Psalm 46.

Reader two:

Silently I sit, silently I pray.
In my heart I feel your peace but I am far away
and all my thoughts are coming from my own point of view
I haven't even tried to hear from you.[3]

---

3   From the song 'Be still' by Dean Allen-Craig. Used by permission.

Reader three:

*I've often sat and wondered if you've a plan
for me
but I never stop to listen
And I am to blind to see your will
Are you trying to speak to me?
Be still, be still.*[4]

Leave some time for silence.

Leader: For any relationship to work, family or friends, there needs to be communication. Not only does there need to be talking, but also active listening. In a relationship with God we need to be silent at times in God's presence. It is possible that there is much to hear.

Reader one: Let us pray, thank you God for this rare time of silence.

Leave some time for silence.

Reader two: Speak to us in the silence.

Leave some time for silence.

Reader three: Help us to continually remember the value of silence. Amen.

Dianne Stevens

4   From the song 'Be still' by Dean Allen-Craig. Used by permission.

THE KINGDOM COMING

You will need:

☐ Candles

☐ Newsprint

☐ Felt pens

PREPARATION

Contact one of the aid agencies in Australia or New Zealand (preferably the Australian/New Zealand Council of Churches or Community Aid Abroad). Ask them for a list of the things that are done through money given to the agency's projects (there are many!).

Darken the room, using only candle-light. Arrange the room so that people will sit in a circle with newsprint and felt pens in the middle.

THE DEVOTION

Begin with some quiet songs, letting the mood of candle-light and darkness quiet the group.

Call the group to worship by using the following prayer:

God, where is this kingdom you have promised?
God, what is this kingdom you have promised?
God, why is the world so different to what you wanted?
God, who will change the world so that

it: feeds the hungry?
clothes the naked?
houses the homeless?
loves the un-lovable?
God, when will things be different?
God, how can things change?
God, who will change the world?

Have each person write down on the newsprint as many things as they want to about the following topic:

● If the world was perfect in every way, what would you have in it? What would it be like?

Leader: When Jesus talked about the Kingdom of God coming on earth, he was talking about a time when things would be perfect. The Kingdom of God is hard to understand, yet it is about a world full of love, no more war, no more hunger.

Have someone read out some of the information you have gathered from the aid agency, outlining what some Christian agencies are doing in the world to usher in God's Kingdom.

Read Matthew 25: 31-45.

What then is the Kingdom of God like? (Have the group brainstorm answers).

Leader: It is hard to be hopeful about the world and the promise of the Kingdom of God, but Christ, before he died reminded the disciples that they were to keep hoping and praying and working for the kingdom. In the meal he shared with them he again promised that the kingdom would come.

Read Luke 22: 14-20.

When the Lord's supper is shared, we remember that the Kingdom of God is coming. It is a message of hope and joy to us and is a reminder that we have a responsibility to respond in any way we can to help bring God's Kingdom on earth.

Finish with some songs about the Kingdom of God.

Mark Beatson,
Leanne and Trevor Ingamels

ISAIAH AND ROCK AND ROLL

You will need:

- [ ] A tape recorder
- [ ] 3 appropriate commercially taped songs (not songs taped from a record)
- [ ] An overhead projector
- [ ] Words of the 3 songs on overhead transparencies
- [ ] 3 readers

PREPARATION

Write up the words of the three songs on the overhead transparencies.

The idea of this devotion is to use current songs in the top 40 to tell the gospel message. Some secular songs that are in the charts have excellent words and a message that corresponds with Christianity. For the purposes of this devotion there are three examples below, which are songs that are not current but should be recognisable.

Choose three themes which may be relevant to young people. For example:

> nuclear warfare
> identity
> justice

Three Bible readings from Isaiah which highlight these themes:

> Isaiah 2: 1-4
> Isaiah 35
> Isaiah 58: 6-12

Three songs which complement these themes are:

'Russians' by Sting (*Dream of the Blue Turtles*)
'Body and Soul' by Jenny Morris (*Body and Soul*)
'Beds are burning' by Midnight Oil (*Diesel and Dust*)

THE DEVOTION

Have everyone sit so they can see the overhead projection screen.

Reader one reads Isaiah 2: 1-4.
The corresponding song is played and displayed on overhead.
The leader leads the group in prayer including:

> Victims of war
> People who live in fear
> The super powers who have the power to destroy
> That the Holy Spirit's peace fills the lives of those who wage war

Reader two reads Isaiah 35.
The corresponding song is played and displayed on overhead.
The leader leads the group in prayer including:

> Asking for help to be people of God
> Asking that we have strength not to conform to the world's standards

Reader three reads Isaiah 58: 6-12.
The corresponding song is played and displayed on overhead.
The leader leads the group in prayer including:

Asking for justice for all people
Especially asking for justice for the original inhabitants of our land
Asking for forgiveness for the times we have been racist
That Aboriginal/Maori people will be able to forgive us for the past and present injustices

Finish the devotion by singing a Christian song about God's love.

Geraldine Anderson

WHO IS JESUS?

You will need:

- [ ] A torch
- [ ] A candle
- [ ] The four phrases (below) written in large letters and put on the wall:
  'JESUS THE REVOLUTIONARY'
  'JESUS THE SUFFERER'
  'JESUS THE LIBERATOR'
  'GOD BECOME HUMAN'

THE DEVOTION

Begin by singing a few appropriate songs about who Jesus is.

Turn out the lights and light the candle

By candlelight read Matthew 16:13-16 and Mark 8: 27-29.

Leader: 'Who do you say I am?' People have asked this question over the centuries and sought to answer it.

(Shine the torch onto the first phrase **'JESUS THE REVOLUTIONARY'**.)

How much for you is Jesus a revolutionary? Is Jesus calling you to turn things upside down, to challenge injustice, to think of new ways of doing things, to make unpopular stands, to challenge others about their attitudes, and to try to change the world and work for the kingdom of God?

How much for you is Jesus a revolutionary?

(Shine the torch onto the second phrase **'JESUS THE SUFFERER'**.)

How much for you is Jesus a sufferer? Calling you to self sacrifice; to support risky causes; to put up with frustration and abuse and ridicule; to give your time to kingdom causes and forgo the money and the things you could have if you put your spare time into looking after yourself rather than trying to care for and help others?

How much for you is Jesus a sufferer?

(Shine the torch onto the third phrase **'JESUS THE LIBERATOR'**.)

How much for you is Jesus a liberator? Calling you to new life, new beginnings, new hope and new freedom; to be open to new ideas; to be a person who lifts burdens from other people and helps them find new meaning in life; to challenge people or structures which constrict the freedom of other people; to help others see that the Christian faith offers new hope and freedom and possibilities, rather than lots of rules.

How much for you is Jesus a liberator?

(Shine the torch onto the fourth phrase **'GOD BECOME HUMAN'**.)

How much for you is Jesus God-become-human? Calling you again and again to focus on God and to make God central to your life, and to devote your entire life to trying to do what you think God wants you to do; who challenges you to point others towards God, and help

©DG 1990

them to keep God at the centre of their lives.

How much for you is Jesus God-become-human?

Give the group five minutes of total silence to reflect on the question:

- 'Who is Jesus for me?'

Finish in prayer:
Lord, help us to keep asking the question and to spend our lives seeking the answer to 'who is Jesus for me'. Amen.

Grant Nichol

BEING BOXED

You will need:

☐ Three or four large boxes (big enough for someone to stand in)

☐ Labels for the boxes (see below)

☐ A cross

PREPARATION

Label your boxes with any labels you choose, below are examples:

Box one—Nerd/Dork/Dag
Box two—Intellectual/Brain
Box three—Trendy/'In'
Box four—Sporty/Athletic

Ask four people to stand in the four boxes and be prepared to answer some questions.

Set the room up so that everyone sits in a circle and the boxes are in the middle, the cross at any point in the circle.

THE DEVOTION

Begin with a few songs about how God loves all of us.

Call the group to worship, asking each person to bring something that is unique to them forward and place it at the cross. The item needs to be something they have with them, it could be a T-shirt, necklace, anything.

Ask the people who you have set up before, to stand in the labelled boxes.

Direct others to spend time at each box finding out at least one thing about the person in the box that they might have in common. Leave enough time for most people to speak to every person in the boxes.

In the large group, discuss how we tend to label people or 'put them in boxes'. Ask each person to tell the rest of the group what label they are often given, or what box they are put in.

Do they like or dislike that label?

Have two or three people read the following Bible readings:

> Matthew 7:1-5
> Romans 2:1
> Romans 12:9-10
> Matthew 5:43-48
> Romans 15:7

Leader: Each person is unique, each person is accepted and loved by God, each person has their own gifts to offer. What is special and unique about you? Tell the person next to you what special or unique thing you brought to the cross.

At the end of the discussion pray an open prayer of confession and thanksgiving: confession about how we label people and judge them, and thanksgiving that all people are unique.

Remember to give back the personal items.

Mark Beatson,
Leanne and Trevor Ingamels.

THE SHAPE OF HEAVEN

You will need:

- [ ] Overhead projector or newsprint and felt pens
- [ ] A cube frame made out of wire
- [ ] Cloth
- [ ] Pencils and paper

PREPARATION

Before the devotion have everyone sit in a circle and place the wire cube, covered with the cloth, in the centre of the circle.

Hand out paper and pencil to each person.

THE DEVOTION

Ask the group what they think heaven is like. List all the ideas on the overhead projector/newsprint.

Leader: There are many ideas in the Bible about what heaven is like. You have provided some of these ideas in the list. Here is a passage that talks about the shape of heaven. Even the shape gives us a clue about what heaven is like.

Have someone read Revelation 21: 9-17. As verses 16 and 17 are being read, uncover the cube.

Leader: The shape of heaven, the city of God, the place where God dwells freely and fully with his people, is a perfect cube. In the cube, all sides and faces are equal; there is no top nor bottom. All relationships within the cube can be understood as horizontal. No one living in the cube is in a dominant position over anyone else. In the cube, no side can claim to be on top. Keeping these images in mind, I invite you to ponder for a minute, the life of Jesus of Nazareth. Jesus was the first person to actually live and die as if the cube of God's Rule had arrived.[5]

What things would have to change in this world for our world to become like the cube? Write those things on your piece of paper.

Leave some time for silence and writing. Have the group drop their pieces of paper into the cube.

Lead a prayer commending those pieces of paper to God.

Finish with an appropriate song about seeking the Kingdom of God.

Mark Lawrence

5   Quoted from a sermon by Ian Williams titled 'The Pyramid and the Cube: Images of Human and Divine Society'. Used with permission.

THE BARN BUILDER

You will need:

- ☐ If possible, a copy of the track 'The Barn Builder' from Ken Medema's *Kingdom in the Streets* album (Word)
- ☐ Another copy of the dramatic Bible reading for a second reader (permission is given to photocopy)
- ☐ Two readers
- ☐ Someone to mime the actions
- ☐ Tape recorder
- ☐ A cardboard box

PREPARATION

You might like to rehearse the dramatic reading with the readers and mime.

THE DEVOTION

This devotion is based on Luke 12: 16-21.

Put the cardboard box at the front or in the middle of the group if you are sitting in a circle.

Explain to the group that inside the box is anything they could possibly wish for. Any possession that they may have always wanted. Give them a few minutes to think about what would be in the box and go around the group asking each person what would be in it for them. When you have asked everyone to contribute, take the box away.

The following dramatised version of the Bible reading is read and acted out.

Two readers—person one and person two. Mime acts as they read.

One: Jesus told lots of stories...

Two: And they had a point to make.

One: He told a story...

Two: About a rich man...

(Enter rich man.)

One: Who had quite a bit of land...

Two: And quite a few crops.

One: He did lots of sowing.

Two: Sow, sow, sow.

One: And lots of reaping.

Two: Reap, reap reap.

One: In fact he did so much sowing and reaping...

Two: Sow, sow, reap, reap...

One: That he didn't have anywhere to keep all his crops.

Two: I have so much food and wealth...

One: He said...

Two: That I must be the wealthiest man around.

One: He realised...

Two: I know what I'll do.

One: He decided...

Two: I'll tear down all my barns.

One: He thought...

Two: And build new, bigger, better barns.

One: Fantastic.

Two: Why didn't I think of that before?

One: Then...

Two: He said...

One: I will say to myself...

Two: Because he was into talking to himself...

One: Oh lucky lucky man

Two: You are so lucky that you have all you need.

One: You are so fortunate.

Two: There is no-one who can hold a candle to you.

One: So, relax...

Two: Have a drink or two...

One: Eat, drink, be merry...

Two: Cheers, clink clink...

One: Sing 'For I'm a jolly good fellow'.

Two: Then in the middle of all this celebrating...

One: God said...

Two: I knew there'd be a catch in this story somewhere...

One: You foolish man.

Two: Foolish?

One: Tonight is the night you will die.

Two: Oh no, gurgle gurgle.

One: And what good will all those riches do for you now?

Two: Oh me, oh my.

One: And then Jesus said...

Two: Coz don't forget that this is Jesus' story...

One: This is how it is with people who pile up riches for themselves...

Two: And are not rich in God's sight.

One: There's no point in trying to buy and own more things...

Two: Because God has better ideas.[6]

Play Ken Medema's 'Barn Builder' song

Place the box back in the middle of the group. Now ask each person to think what God would place in the box for us. Give some time for thought, then go around the group and ask each person to contribute.

Commend all the thoughts to God in prayer.

Geraldine Anderson

---

6   This style of 'adapted reading' comes from the British drama writers Paul Burbridge and Murray Watts. Their two books: *Lightning Sketches* and *Time to Act* are good resources for devotions. The books are published by Hodder and Stoughton.

SHOES SHINE

You will need:

☐ A person who will read the Bible reading.

THE DEVOTION

Have each person remove a shoe and place in a pile in the middle of the room.

People then pair off and they must find the other person's shoe.

Each person takes turns in explaining what the shoe says about the owner. Then the person responds about how accurate that person was in his/her judgement.

Leader: Psychologists say that shoes are a very important piece of clothing, as people look down at our feet rather than up at us (eye to eye). Shoes therefore can be a statement of who we are and how we want to be seen.

In the same pairs answer the following question:

- What sort of footwear is symbolic of how we see ourselves? (i.e., what sort of shoes show the type of person you are?)

Read the poem 'The Lived Life'[7] on page 41.

Have someone read Matthew 6: 25-33.

Again in their pairs ask the people to talk about how the poem relates to Jesus' words in the Bible reading.

Conclude in open prayer. Each time a person finishes a prayer, everyone in the group must click their heels together once as a sign of agreement.

David Guthrey

7   Reprinted from *Bless my Growing* by Gerhard E. Frost, copyright © 1974 Augsburg Publishing House. Used by permission of Augsburg Fortress.

I remember a little pair of shoes.
For months they stood side by side
on the closet floor,
begging for feet.

We had an active four year old
who ran and danced through the days
with always new plans for the morrow.
But one day she lay still
in a distant hospital
while the weeks went by.
It was polio.

We had shopped for shoes
and she loved hers especially
because they were her first that tied
I remember praying as we put them aside
that they would be worn again.

That experience taught me
that it is high privilege
to support life.
Never since have I complained
about the price of children's shoes.
Life is meant to beget and sustain more life
To grow tired is not tragedy
if one is living by loving,
dying by giving.

The call to discipleship
is to 'come and die',
usually not in one burst of effort
or in a single pool of blood
but in the steady self-draining
of life-strength and energy.

There is no room for self-pity
in the lived life
Only the unlived quality of our existence
should ever make us sad.

SELF ESTEEM

You will need:

☐ Newsprint

☐ Felt pens

☐ Pencils and paper for everyone

PREPARATION

Be familiar with the diagrams at the foot of the page so that you can explain them to the group.

THE DEVOTION

Hand out pencils and paper And ask the group to draw a horizontal line on their page with the numbers one to ten spaced evenly along the line (see diagram 1).

Leader: Self esteem is the picture you have of yourself which tells you what you are like. It tells you what you are good and bad at, and what other people think of you. If you have a strong self esteem then you have a strong belief in yourself that you are OK, that you are competent, lovable and deserving of respect from people you know.

If you have a low self esteem you may think of yourself as ugly, stupid, dull, un-lovely and incompetent. If 'Low self esteem' was on the left of the line you have drawn (near 1) and 'Strong self esteem was at the right of the line (near 10), where would you mark yourself on that line?

When they have finished marking their line, break them up into groups of three. Then ask the following questions:

- Share your line and where you put your mark.

Diagram 1:

| 1 | 2 | 3 | 4 | 5 | 6 | 7 | 8 | 9 | 10 |

Diagram 2:

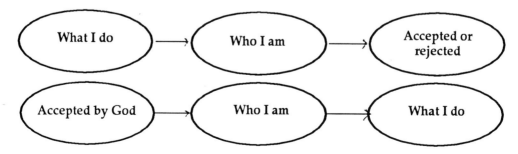

- How does this affect the way you live?
- Do you have control over self esteem?

Leader: Here is a diagram which represents a widely held theory on how our self esteem level works.

As you talk, write up on the newsprint the first line from diagram 2 (What I do Who I am Accepted or rejected).

In Australia and New Zealand, people tend to identify more strongly with what they cannot do, rather than what they can do. In identifying with things we cannot do, we see ourselves as non-achievers and therefore end up with a low self esteem.

Put downs and sarcasm is a great Australian and New Zealand pastime. What effect do you think this would have on people? *(Ask people to yell out what they think.)*

If we are seeking to increase our self esteem, one thing we should do is to learn to identify more strongly with things we can do and see ourselves in the light of our achievements. Think for a minute about what your personal strengths are.

(Leave some time for silent thought.)

Pray a prayer of thanksgiving for gifts and strengths.

Have some readers read:

> Genesis 1: 27-28
> Psalm 8: 3-6
> Isaiah 40:11
> John 3:16

Leader: God sees us as lovable, capable, wonderful beings, therefore the diagram that I drew before would be changed as far as God is concerned.

Complete the diagram on the newsprint while you are talking (Accepted by God Who I am What I do).

Notice that 'Who I am' and 'What I do' are now determined by what God thinks of us. The world says we are accepted or rejected by who we are and what we do. God says 'you are accepted', and who you are and what you do all comes from the fact that you are loved and needed.

Think about that next time the world wants to tell you who you are. You are God's.

Finish with some songs or a prayer.

John Brown

DEATH AND LIFE CELEBRATION

You will need

- [ ] A free standing wooden cross
- [ ] Paper, pencils, balloons (enough for each person)
- [ ] Streamers (enough for one between two)
- [ ] Felt pens
- [ ] A tape recorder
- [ ] A piece of celebration music, for example 'The Easter Song' by Keith Green or the 'Hallelujah Chorus', or any other piece you think would help people celebrate.

PREPARATION

This devotion goes best after Easter.

Put the group into a circle and place the free standing cross in the middle of the circle. Hand out pencil and paper, balloons and streamers before you begin the devotion.

THE DEVOTION

Explain that this devotion will follow, to some degree the Easter story.

Read from Matthew 27: 45-50.

Ask the group to think about things today which are symbols of crucifixion. What things in our world are bad and seem hopeless?

Each person then writes those things on their piece of paper in silence and the pieces of paper are attached to the cross.

Read Matthew 27: 57-61.

A reflective song may be sung here.

Read Matthew 28: 1-10.

Ask people to think about signs of hope and joy they see in the world: things that are symbols of the resurrection.

Each person blows up their balloon and writes with a felt pen, those symbols of hope, joy and resurrection. The balloons are then attached to the cross over the pieces of paper.

Leader: Jesus Christ suffered and died at the hands of the people of the world. Today the world still 'crucifies' Christ by being the way it is—for example the things we have written on our pieces of paper. The good news is that Jesus Christ rose from the dead and gave us hope that the world can be a better place. The cross of death is covered with our symbols of resurrection and new life. There is hope and new life with Jesus.

The people are asked to stand in a circle and while the music is playing, those who have streamers throw them at the cross.

When the music has finished, as an act of sending each other out, the people are asked to greet each other with the words: 'Jesus Christ is risen' and the answer 'he is risen indeed'.

Sue Clarkson

SEEING IT

You will need

☐ Large frame

☐ White sheet

☐ Overhead projector

☐ 4 or 5 people to mime the story

☐ Bread

PREPARATION

The idea of this devotion is to let the Easter story speak for itself by using mime. The sheet, frame and overhead projector are used as stage props. The sheet is stretched over the frame and the overhead projector placed behind it and turned on so that the light will silhouette any action that happens onto the sheet.

This needs to be rehearsed but not to any great extent.

THE DEVOTION

Sit the group at one long table. Loaves of bread are placed within reach of the people. They are all facing one way—towards the sheet on the frame.

A person with good reading skills then reads the Easter story. As the reader reads, the actors mime the action behind the screen. The following extracts of the Easter story are suggested.

Part 1: Matthew 26: 26-30
Props: Table behind screen

Part 2: Matthew 26: 36-46
Props: Branch of tree behind screen

Part 3: Matthew 26: 47-56
Props: Swords in actors' hands

Part 4: Matthew 27: 1-2
Props: Chains

Part 5: Matthew 27: 15-26
Props: Bowl, water

Part 6: Matthew 27: 32-44
Props: cross, cup, nails, hammer

Part 7: Matthew 27: 45-50
Props: same as above

Part 8: Matthew 27: 57-61
Props: large stone/rock

Part 9: Matthew 28: 1-10
Props: same as above

The devotion can be finished with singing, prayer, or perhaps some discussion about what has taken place. As the devotion is mostly passive, some discussion may be helpful.

Sue Clarkson

ON THE ROAD

You will need:

☐ Someone to read the Bible

☐ Someone to do the prayers

PREPARATION

This devotion requires that you walk around outside. You will need a smaller group to do this, as in a large group the words will be lost.

THE DEVOTION

Gather the group and encourage them to walk close to you and the reader.

You begin walking with the group.

Reader reads Luke 24:13-16.

Leader: This is happening after Jesus has been crucified. The disciples are confused and upset, the Messiah they thought was going to save them was dead. In no way were they expecting to meet Jesus. They were unhappy, angry, disbelieving and worried. And Jesus came to them.

When you are upset, worried, angry and disbelieving, does Jesus come to you without you knowing it?

Reader reads Luke 24: 17-24.

Leader: Jesus came without barging in, he came, listened to the story and heard their version of what was happening.

The prayer prays:

Dear Lord Jesus, forgive us when we barge in on people and fill them with our news and who we are. Help us to listen more, to be sensitive to other people and to learn from your example. Help us to join with people, hear their story, and listen with our hearts and heads.

Reader reads Luke 24: 25-27.

Leader: Jesus reminds us that we often have heard the message he gives but are unwilling to believe it.

Leave some time for silence.

Reader reads Luke 24: 28-29.

Leader: Jesus responded to the invitation to stay and talk. How often have we run away from opportunities to talk about God.

Prayer prays:

Dear Lord Jesus, forgive us for not making the most of opportunities that come our way. We would like to offer ourselves to you, but sometimes we are too frightened. Give us strength to do your will and be your disciples.

Reader reads Luke 24: 30-35.

Leader: In the breaking of the bread, the disciples recognised Jesus. Perhaps it reminded them of the last time Jesus had broken bread. The followers raced back to Jerusalem to tell their story. They had met Jesus on the road and were so excited that they couldn't wait to tell their friends. Pass the peace of Jesus

Christ amongst yourselves. One person says 'The peace of the Lord Jesus be with you' and the other person replies 'and also with you'.

Sing a song the group will be familiar with as you walk back to where you started from.

Dianne Stevens and Grant Nichol

IT WASN'T EASY

You will need:

☐ A copy of the Petra song 'It is finished' from their album *This means war*.

☐ Three inch nails with pieces of paper attached to them (enough for one per person)

☐ Hammer

☐ Pens

☐ A wooden cross

THE DEVOTION

Leader: Crucifixion was a very painful and degrading way to die. Death was slow and incredibly taxing physically. Death was by slow suffocation, caused by the shoulder muscles gradually giving way, the chest being compressed. Hammering nails into a persons hands or wrists was an optional torture.

This is the way Jesus died. Jesus was aware of this outcome, but went ahead anyway. What those executioners did then is similar to the things we do now, we hurt Jesus by our actions of jealousy, aggression, bitterness.

Read Matthew 27: 45-50.

List the things in your life which hold you down from your family, from your friends, from God. List them on the piece of paper attached to the nail you have been given.

When they have done this, have them bring their nail forward and someone will hammer it onto the cross.

While the hammering is going on ask everyone to stand and hold their arms out, hands straight out, feet slightly bent. This is the pose of the crucifixion and they are to stay this way until the song 'It is finished' by Petra is finished (it runs for about four minutes). The hammering should still be going on.

When the song is finished, assure the group of God's forgiveness, and tear off the papers from the nails on the cross. Explain that we worship a risen lord. Therefore the cross is empty.

Conclude with a spoken or sung benediction.

Glen Elliott and David Guthrey

UNDER ARREST

(suitable for 12-14/15 year olds)

You will need:

☐ Paper handcuffs for each person.
(Prepare two strips of paper 25mm wide 200mm long, link them and staple them)

☐ A small cross on a table

PREPARATION

Plan to have your devotion in a different room/place.

THE DEVOTION

As people arrive 'handcuff' everyone. (Be careful as they are only paper and will break easily.)

Sing some praise songs as a call to worship. After the singing ask people to pass the peace amongst themselves (with their handcuffs on).

Have someone read John 8: 31-41.

Ask the group to brainstorm things in our lives that make us feel as if we are 'under arrest' or in bondage, e.g.:

selfishness
peer group pressure
family

In a time of silence, have each person pray quietly to themselves about those things in their lives. End the silence by reading John 8:36.

Have everyone snap their handcuffs off, screw up the paper and come forward and place the paper at the foot of the cross.

Finish by singing some praise songs, especially songs about freedom in Christ.

Steve Campbell

GRAFFITI

(suitable for 12-14/15 year olds)

You will need:

- ☐ Large sheet of newsprint with a brick wall drawn on it
- ☐ Felt pens

THE DEVOTION

Give the group some time to think about what/who God is. Then ask them to go up to the brick 'graffiti' wall you have drawn and write the words that come to mind when they think of God.

Draw attention to the 'graffiti wall' when all people have written on it. Highlight some of the words people have written.

Have someone read Genesis 1: 26-31.

Ask the group to go back to the 'graffiti wall' and circle words on the wall that describe them. If we are made in God's image, then what qualities of God's do we have? Ask that they do this in silence.

When they have finished this have each person sit apart from everyone else. At this point you might like to have some music which will help people think.

Ask each person to think of two things about themselves that they think would please God. For example they may be patient, or caring. After some time, pray a prayer of thanksgiving for gifts we have and a prayer of challenge, asking that God never lets us rest, but keep striving to be faithful disciples.

As a final act, invite everyone to go to the 'graffiti wall' and tear a piece off for themselves. Encourage them to take the piece home and keep it somewhere to remind them they are made in God's image.

Mark Beatson,
Leanne and Trevor Ingamels

WHO CARES?

CAUTION

This devotion is designed to challenge people and has material within it that may make your group uncomfortable. Please be aware of that and change things if necessary.

THE DEVOTION

Divide the people into groups of three or four. Ask them to come up with what they would call a great 'clean' joke. After a few minutes, give people a chance to tell the joke to the rest of the group.

The following 'joke' is an example of the type of humour that is expressed in many areas of our society. The nationalities of the three on the cliff are made up, but you will know the nationalities within this country that people abuse. It is in the form of a question:

Question: 'If a Creptokian, an Ingletan, and a Davildon were on the top of a cliff and they all jumped off, who would land on the ground first?'

Answer: 'Who cares?'

Ask people how this 'joke' makes them feel. Have them call out their responses to the group.

Ask the group why we make up things like this and call them 'jokes'.

Read Matthew 27: 27-31.

Leader: It is not a new thing that people are mocked and jeered at for who they are or what they look like or what they do and believe. And when any one of God's children is mocked and jeered at, then Christ suffers as well. The answer to the question in the 'joke' is who cares? The Bible assures us that God cares, God suffered and died at the hands of the mocking crowd, God knows what it means to be persecuted.

Read Galatians 3: 26-29.

Back in the groups they were in before, ask them to discuss what that Bible passage might mean for today.

Leader: The question is 'Who cares?' Do we care enough about our world to try to make it good for all people to live in? Do we care about people no matter who they are, what they do or what they look like?
It isn't funny not to care. Where do you stand?

Finish with a prayer. You might like to open the prayer to the group so that they can pray their own prayers.

Trudi Sharp

WE ARE THE CHURCH

You will need:

☐ Religious symbols from different Christian churches, e.g.
crucifix (cross with Jesus on it)
picture of Mary, mother of Jesus
icon
empty cross

PREPARATION

Gather as much information as you can about other denominations so that you are able to speak with some authority if you are asked questions.

Place the religious symbols at the front, spaced apart.

THE DEVOTION

Read 1 Corinthians 12: 1-28a.

Leader: Usually when we read this reading we relate it to how we all have different talents and contributions to make in our group, or our church. However, lets read it thinking about the whole church community. All the different denominations like Catholic, Orthodox, Anglican, Uniting Church, Presbyterian, Methodist, Churches of Christ, Baptist, Lutheran belong to the world church and we all worship the one God.

Look at these items from other denominations at the front. What do these things symbolise for you? (Pick up each item and leave some silence.)

Then explain what each symbol is and what it means to its denomination. If appropriate, you could pass the items around so that people could touch them.

Then read the following:

1 Corinthians 12: 14-20—paraphrased

For the world church itself is not made up of only one part, but of many parts. If the Anglicans were to say, 'Because we are not Baptists we do not belong to the world church', that would not keep it from being part of the world church. And if the Uniting Church were to say, 'Because we are not Lutherans, we do not belong to the world church', that would not keep it from being a part of the world church. If the whole world church were just Catholics or Churches of Christ, everything would be all the same, how would it cater for people who wanted different things? There are many parts but one body.

Pray, asking for understanding and tolerance. Give thanks for the diversity of the churches. Pray that we don't fear different people with different beliefs.

You might like to sing some songs from Taize, which is a Christian community in France, which is non-denominational. Taize chants are in Latin, so that the one language is used. You will find music from Taize in any Christian book shop.

Heather McMinn

DRY BONES

You will need:

- ☐ Bones (either animal or if you know a medical student who has a skeleton that might be helpful)
- ☐ Fan
- ☐ Red and silver streamers
- ☐ Clay
- ☐ Candles (one for each person)

PREPARATION

Prepare the room in the following way:

Put the bones in one corner with lumps of clay around them.
In another corner place the fan with the streamers attached to it.

The way this devotion will proceed is that people will move from one corner to another as the devotion goes on.

THE DEVOTION

First corner:

At the corner with the bones, have some-one read Ezekial 37: 1-4.

Leader: These dry bones are like us when our spirit is weak. Think of times when you have felt like a bag of dry bones. When things have not gone well for you. Yell out the feelings this brings out.

Sing a song asking for God's spirit to come.

Second corner:

Have people move to a corner of the room that has nothing in it.

Read John 15: 26-27.

Leader: When have you received help in your life. When things have been bad, has someone helped you, have you felt 'a helper' in your life?

Leave some time for silence.

Pray a prayer of thanksgiving, ask the group to join in by shouting out one or two word prayers of thanks.

Third corner:

Have people move to the corner of the room where the fan is set up with the streamers coming from it. Turn on the fan and instruct people to sit down.

Read Acts 2: 1-22.

Ask the people to turn to the person next to them and answer the question:

- What does it mean to be filled with the Spirit?

Sing a song about the Spirit being like wind.

Fourth corner

Return to the first corner where the bones are. Hand out small candles to everyone. Firstly light your own candle saying:

'The fire, the light is a sign of the Spirit, the sign of life. Come and light your candle from this candle and place it in the clay which is amongst the bones. In this way we will place the Spirit's fire and life amongst the bones.'

As the people are coming forward and placing their lit candle in the clay read:

Ezekial 37: 4-14.

When people have finished, have the group join hands and form a circle. Ask each person to silently pray for the person on their right, that they be empowered with the spirit, that they always know they are not alone.

You might like to finish with a sung benediction.

Heather McMinn and Leonie Purcival

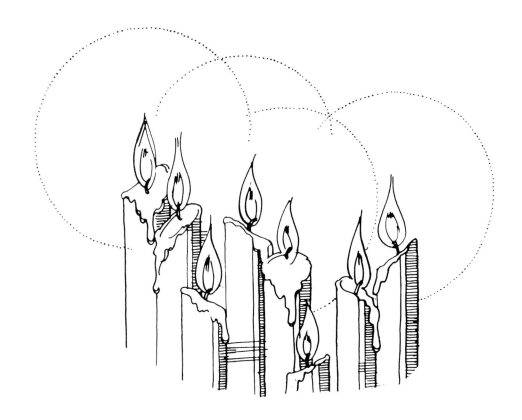

NOWHERE TO LAY HIS HEAD

THE DEVOTION

Read the story in the box on this page.

Once there was a young man who had nowhere to live. Through no fault of his own, he had nowhere to lay his head. Whenever people saw him, they avoided him, not because he was rude or violent, but because people tend to be scared of anyone who looks like they are lonely or have no money. The young man had no money, very few clothes and no home.

The people would talk about him in scandalised tones. 'Who is this vagrant, who wanders the streets and appears to have nowhere to go? He hangs around the public areas and talks to people. He's a bad influence on our children', they said. Some people even thought it would be best to run him out of town.

Very few people thought it would be a good idea to ask why he had nowhere to go, or perhaps ask him home to their own houses. People used to do that years ago, but pretty soon the number of homeless people seemed to increase and it was decided that if you started to give homeless people homes, then more people would deliberately become homeless to 'bludge' off your charity.

So the young man remained home-less, with nowhere to lay his head, and the people began to plot against him.

There was a girl in the town who was something of an academic. She knew what to do about the young man. She said she had been reading an ancient book that talked about a similar vagrant young man who had nowhere to live, who wandered from place to place and talked to people wherever he went. The girl and her family promised to deal with the situation.

They found some wood and they made a cross; they got some nails and they took the young man out and nailed his hands and feet to the cross. 'This is how they got rid of the vagrant thousands of years ago', said the girl. 'There is stacks to learn from this book', she said as she waved it in the air.

Someone else picked up the book and read aloud from it: 'Foxes have holes, and birds have nests, but the Son of Man has nowhere to lie down and rest.' The people were glad that the ancient book had something to say about vagrants and homeless people. After all they didn't want to do anything that was wrong, and the book justified what they did. Pretty soon, people with nowhere to lie down and rest stopped coming to that town, and the ancient book was praised for its wisdom.

Leave some time for silence.

Pray the following prayer:

Creator God, forgive us for ignoring the homeless
Forgive us for mocking the poor
Forgive us for avoiding the lonely
Forgive us for turning away the hungry
Creator God, forgive us for crucifying

you again
When we ignore, mock, avoid and turn away from your children.

Read Matthew 8:20.

Finish with a song.

Rod Samuels

IF I HAD A CHANCE

You will need:

☐ Pencils and paper (enough for each group—see below)

THE DEVOTION

Read the reflection in the box:

Break into small groups of three or four. Ask the groups to write prayers beginning 'If I had a chance...' Explain that they are to think about what they would do, given the chance about any aspect of this world. When you have given enough time, bring them back into the large group.

Ask each group to present the prayers they have written. Between each prayer, the leader should say:

Jesus said: 'These things are impossible for human beings, but with God, all things are possible' (Matthew 19:26).

When the prayers are over, finish by singing some songs about the might and wonder of God.

> If I had a chance to speak to the leaders of this world I wouldn't say anything at first. But I'd put them all in a room and I would take with me a new born baby. I would take that baby around and show each of the world leaders the tiny form. I'd tell them:
>
> 'Study this child, you world leaders, see the freedom of its movements, watch the hands clench and un-clench, hear the soft breathing and see the peaceful way it sleeps.'
>
> 'Study this child, you people who make bombs and have economic policies that hurt the poor. Study this child and remember that this is the child your bombs and policies will kill, maim, starve and torture. This is the child of Africa, Asia, South America, this is the child of Ireland and this is an Aboriginal child.'
>
> 'Remember, you world leaders, when you make your bombs and your policies that it is the innocent, like this child who you attack.'

Geraldine Anderson

GLUE

(suitable for 12-14/15 year olds)

You will need:

☐ Pot or a tube of glue

THE DEVOTION

Begin by telling a story of your own about a time when you broke something valuable. If you don't have a story of your own, use the following:

'When I was small, I was drying the dishes with my mother. She had a favourite cup. It was a special cup commemorating the coronation of Queen Elizabeth II. Unfortunately I was a little clumsy and dropped it onto our stone floor. It broke into hundreds of pieces. In my defence I told my mother I'd fix it. I ran into my bedroom and returned to the kitchen with a pot of glue. My mother, however, was unimpressed. The cup was too badly broken to be fixed with ordinary glue.' (Show the pot of ordinary glue you have.)

Ask people in the group to contribute a story (two or three would be sufficient).

Leader: A Canadian poet once said that God is like glue. What do you think God is like? (Spend some time brainstorming what the group think God is like.)

There are three reasons why this Canadian poet thought God was like glue.

1. God is like glue in that God made the world. It is sustained, it is kept running by God. God holds it all together, the Universe didn't just sort of happen.

2. God promised, through Jesus, to stick with us no matter what. God sticks with us when others might desert us or let us down. God promises to stay with us.

3. Sometimes when we get broken or hurt through grief, failure, disappointment, illness, criticism, it is God who can help put us together again. God is a great fixer, a great healer and restorer.

Sing some appropriate songs about God the creator, God being with us, or God the healer.

Finish with the following prayer:

Loving God, thank you for the beautiful world you have made. Please help us care for it.
Thank you for your life-giving presence and the many ways you want to make us whole and new, through Jesus Christ, Amen.

Steve Francis

THE STARS AND ALL THAT

You will need:

☐ It is suggested that you use the music from the movies *The Mission* (the first track) and *Star Wars* (the theme music). However if you do not have access to this music, some meditative and then dramatic classical music would suffice.

PREPARATION

This devotion is best held outside, on a cloudless night, when the stars are visible. It is not absolutely necessary, but will enhance what is done.

THE DEVOTION

Ask everyone to lie down on the ground (or the floor) and get comfortable (not so comfortable that they fall asleep). Explain that there will be a time of reflection. The first part will be some input and the second part will be for individual prayer. Ask people to relax, stop fidgeting, and when reasonable quiet is achieved, begin.

Leader: When you look up at the stars, what thoughts come into your head?

What is it that the stars have that sometimes holds us mesmerised. Throughout time, stars have always been significant. Stars even defeat time at its own battle. When we look up we are seeing the images of heavenly bodies that may have ceased to exist more than 1000 years ago.

Stars have long been put to practical use as well. Navigation was once near impossible without the aid of the stars. People use the stars to direct their lives and it was a special star that led important people to a small stable in Bethlehem. The coming of that star changed everyone's lives for ever.

Read Matthew 2: 1-2, then Psalm 8.

The stars are an example of the size and the greatness of God. When we look at the sky at night, we can become over-awed. Our minds cannot comprehend the magnitude of it all, the sky is so large, we are told it is infinite. Yet we can see the stars; we believe in the stars.

It is the same with trying to comprehend who and what God is. How can we imagine the being that created something as complex as the stars? How can we begin to understand? What was there before God?

As I play some music, please think what and who God is, think about how God has a part to play in your life. Spend the time in prayer.

Allow at least five or six minutes, or until the music you have stops.

Finish with a song or two.

Jason Wright

I STILL HAVEN'T FOUND WHAT I'M LOOKING FOR

You will need:

- [ ] Cut out photographs, magazine pictures, newspaper pictures of young people (enough for one picture per person).

- [ ] The song 'I still haven't found what I'm looking for' by U2, from both the *Joshua Tree* album and *Rattle and Hum* by U2.

PREPARATION

Arrange the room so that people will sit in a circle and lay all the pictures you have cut out on the floor in the middle of the circle.

THE DEVOTION

Ask each person to look at the pictures of young people in the middle of the floor. They may get up and walk around to get a good look at the pictures.

Ask each person to pick a picture that reminds them most of themselves.

In pairs or groups of three, have the people share why they chose the picture they did and why it reminds them of themselves.

Leader: There are two Bible readings about Thomas, who was a disciple of Jesus that we will read. Thomas was a lot like many young people. Listen to the two sides of Thomas.

Just after Jesus has heard his friend Lazarus has died, he says he is going to where Lazarus has died and will be buried, which is near Jerusalem, at Bethany. His disciples are scared because going to Jerusalem seems like suicide to them. The authorities in Jerusalem were after Jesus.

But Thomas is all 'gung-ho' and fired up, ready to go with Jesus, even to death.

(Either read or have someone else read John 11:16.)

Later on, after the death and resurrection of Jesus, we hear about the Thomas we are all much more familiar with.

(Either read or have someone else read John 20: 24-29.)

This is the Thomas who doesn't believe anything unless he can physically prove it.

Many young people, like you, are like Thomas—sometimes sure about faith, other times disbelieving. People your age change so much physically and mentally as they grow up and they learn so much. They are challenged and have many new experiences. With regard to Christian faith, it is a time of doubt and searching and working out who they are and what life is about. And not only young people are like Thomas, not only young people have doubts.

I'm going to play a song by U2 who are an Irish band and are also Christians.

While you listen to the song. Think about faith and where you are at in your faith.

Play the song.

Then pray the following prayer:

Creator God, faith is a life journey which never finishes. It gives some answers which always raises more questions. Our faith drives us on, keeps us on the journey, keeps us seeking. Christian faith doesn't mean we've arrived, but we keep looking and we never find exactly what we're looking for—as we find some answers—they always raise more questions and we have to keep looking, secure in the knowledge that you love us and the power of the spirit will keep us going. Amen.

Grant Nichol

THE INVITATION

You will need:

☐ Prepared invitations (see example below) names can be written in at the last minute

☐ A good sized cross made out of cardboard and covered with clear contact

☐ One water based felt pen (very important that it is water based)

☐ Wet sponge

PREPARATION

Sometime before the time of devotion, hand out an invitation to each person.

THE INVITATION

The invitation on the opposite page is an example of what you can use—you might like to invent your own.

THE DEVOTION

Start with a welcome and some singing of your favourite songs

Have someone read Luke 14: 15-25.

Leader: Every one of us receives an invitation from Jesus, inviting us to be part of the Christian family, to be a disciple of Christ. It is up to us whether we respond or not. We often respond conditionally, depending on the circumstances around us. Think of at at least one thing that stops you from accepting the invitation to follow Christ, to become a Christian. It could be a range of things, for example:

- Embarrassed to be a Christian because of what others will think
- Can't believe in what the Christian faith teaches
- Don't want to have to change my life-style

After some silence, invite people to come forward and write their barrier on the cross with the water based pen you have provided.

When all who want to write have written on the cross, use the sponge to wipe the writing off. While doing this it should be highlighted that Jesus Christ died on the cross so that our sins will be forgiven and also so that we may never again be held back from having a relationship with God. State that Jesus can take these obstacles away.

Finish in a time of open prayer in which you invite the members to pray.

Steve Campbell

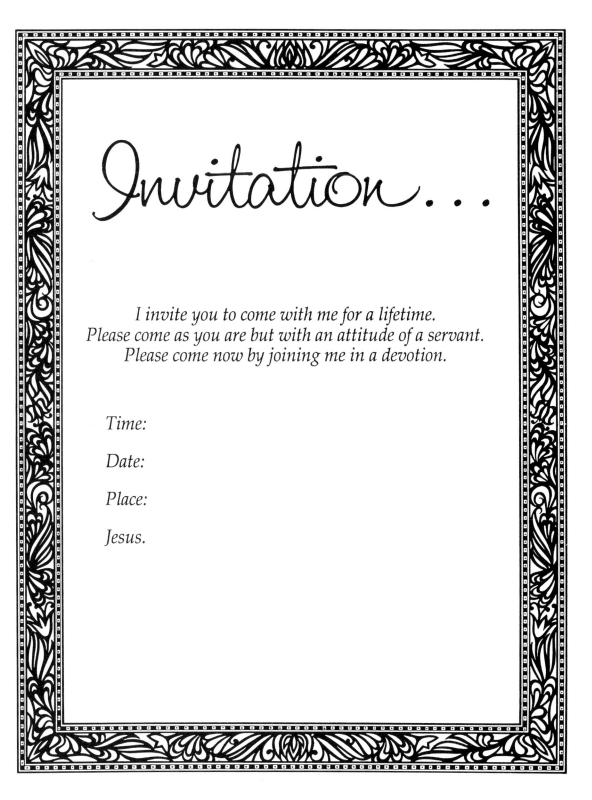

Invitation . . .

I invite you to come with me for a lifetime.
Please come as you are but with an attitude of a servant.
Please come now by joining me in a devotion.

Time:

Date:

Place:

Jesus.

CHINESE WHISPERS

You will need:

☐ Someone to read the Bible reading

THE DEVOTION

Ask everyone to sit on the floor in a circle. Explain that you are going to play chinese whispers. You will start a sentence and whisper it to one person. They in turn will whisper what they heard to the person next to them.

Make the first one quite easy and about something basic like:

> The carpet here is blue and the walls are also blue.

The last person to hear the sentence is to repeat it aloud to the group. There shouldn't be too much difference in the first one.

Then make the message more complex and this time make up a fictional person for example:

Joe Bloggs was seen stealing something from the local shop. He is in trouble with the police and he might have to go to jail. His parents are very upset.

See how that comes out when it's been through the group. Usually the message is distorted or exaggerated by the time it has been whispered from one person to the next.

Ask the group:

- Has anyone ever gossiped about you or told people things that aren't really true about you?
  What was it like?
- Do you ever talk about people without knowing the real facts?

Read Psalm 34: 11-14.

Pray an open prayer asking for forgiveness for times when our tongues have hurt other people.

Finish by singing some songs.

Wendy McKenzie

DO IT YOURSELF

You will need:

☐ Your own creativity. Follow the model set out below and the notes on devotions in the introduction to help write your own devotion.

MY DEVOTION

1. BIBLE/FOCUS What issue is to be focused upon?
What reading will be used to highlight that issue?
How can you find out what young people see as real issues?

2. MEDIUM In what way will you raise the issue (song, drama, posters, talk, role playing etc). Bible reading at this point.

3. IDENTIFYING Do individuals have an opportunity to identify with the issue—individually or corporately? eg., prayer, small group discussion, time for silent reflection.

4. RESPONSE Do individuals have an opportunity to respond to what has been raised eg., prayer, small group discussion, sculpture, their own offering?

5. EVALUATION

- Did the devotion work?
- What did/what didn't work?
- Are there any other issues to be looked at that have been raised in this devotion?
- What would be changed to make this a better devotion the next time I use it?

David Guthrey